Original title:
The Call of the Tropics

Copyright © 2025 Creative Arts Management OÜ
All rights reserved.

Author: Olivia Sterling
ISBN HARDBACK: 978-1-80581-486-3
ISBN PAPERBACK: 978-1-80581-013-1
ISBN EBOOK: 978-1-80581-486-3

Echoes of the Past in Forgotten Shores

On sandy beaches, crabs in suits,
They shuffle sideways, clumsy brutes.
Old shells whisper tales of yore,
Of pirate treasure and sea turtle lore.

Seagulls squawk like they own the place,
Diving down with elegant grace.
Yet all they find is a sandwich left,
Sprouting lettuce—oh, the theft!

Where Every Leaf Tells a Story

In jungles thick, leaves gossip loud,
Sharing secrets in a leafy crowd.
Frogs wear crowns like royalty,
While monkeys jest in pure loyalty.

Chameleons boast their changing looks,
Reading nature's well-worn books.
Each rustling leaf, a silly tale,
Of frogs who dreamed to sail and sail.

The Legacies of Sun and Rain

The sun shines bright, with a cheeky grin,
While raindrops dance, let the fun begin.
Flowers giggle beneath the sun,
Playing hide and seek—oh, it's such fun!

A coconut falls with a thud and a splash,
While toucans flaunt their colors like cash.
In this bright world, nothing is sour,
Except the lemons—what a quirky flower!

Embracing the Wild Side of Nature

Lions lounge while parrots squawk,
The wildlife holds quite the talk.
Sloths take naps with a daily schedule,
Living life at a slothful level.

Trees join in with a rustling cheer,
Swaying side to side, the rhythm's clear.
Nature's a party, let's all get wild,
With laughter and joy, just like a child!

Wildflowers in Abandon

In fields where wildflowers spin and twirl,
Dandelions dance, give the bees a whirl.
A cactus wearing shades, so proud and bright,
Laughs at the sun, oh what a quirky sight!

Butterflies on vacation, sipping sweet tea,
Chasing one another, 'Oh look, there's me!'
With petals waving high, they throw a spree,
Saying 'Life's a garden, come join the glee!'

The Pulse of Rainforest Rhythms

In the jungle, monkeys play, swing and screech,
While sloths in slow-mo make it out of reach.
A parrot's gossip spouts, so loud and clear,
'He's been eating all my fruits, I shed a tear!'

Frogs croak serenades, a croaky choir,
While ants march on parade, their tiny empire.
Bamboo sways like a dancer, full of grace,
In this rhythm of life, there's no need for space.

Dawn over Emerald Isles

Morning breaks with a splash, waves tickle toes,
Seagulls gossip, 'Did you see that? Who knows!'
Palm trees sway like they've hit the fun zone,
'Last night's breeze? A bit too overblown!'

Sandy footprints lead to merry bandits,
Crabs in tiny tuxedos, quite the finds!
With coconuts for helmets, they march ahead,
'We're kings of this island, watch us, no dread!'

Nectar of Flora and Fauna

Bees buzz in the meadow, plotting sweet fame,
Sipping on nectar, like it's a game.
A flower blushing pink, quite the show-off,
'Honey, I bloom best when you're feeling soft!'

The ants march along, with snacks in their gear,
'Is it lunch already? Oh, let's gather near!'
Caterpillars chuckle, spinning tales so bold,
'Soon we'll fly high, just wait till we're gold!'

The Artisan's Palm Frond

In the sun, the craftsman grins,
With palm fronds dancing in the breeze,
He shapes a hat for folks with chins,
And jokes about his stubby knees.

A lady asks for something fine,
He crafts a purse that's full of flair,
But then he trips on his own line,
And laughs while fixing up his hair.

A bird swoops down with quite a flair,
He steals the hat before it lands,
The artisan just stands in stare,
And swears he's working with his hands.

With winks and nods, they toss their trade,
In bright array, they laugh and jest,
For in the shade, where toil is made,
It's all a game, and they're the best.

Breath of the Tropics

A monkey swings from vine to vine,
He glances back, and then he grins,
He snatches fruits, a playful line,
Reminds us all of silly sins.

The breeze comes in with giggling sounds,
It teases flowers, makes them sway,
While lizards sun on warming grounds,
Planning for a lazy day.

And then a parrot joins the fray,
With colors bright that catch the eye,
He squawks a tune in disarray,
As folks just laugh and wonder why.

In this warm place, where joy is rife,
Life's just a game of funny chance,
Amidst the heat, the zest of life,
We dance along, in wild expanse.

Sanctuary of the Feathered Friends

In leafy realms where laughter sings,
The birds all gather, bright and gay,
With gossip shared on buzzing wings,
    As playful jests adorn the day.

A pigeon shows off all his moves,
While sparrows giggle from afar,
The parakeets have tunes to prove,
That life can twirl like a twinkling star.

One feathered friend, a true delight,
Tells tales of worms and sunny skies,
The others laugh till it feels right,
As laughter echoes, birds all rise.

In branches thick, the fun won't end,
For every chirp's a joke in flight,
This sanctuary, silly blend,
Is where the world feels just so bright.

A Palette of Flora and Song

In gardens bright, a blooms parade,
With colors splashed like paints in spring,
Each petal wakes and hums a trade,
While laughter drifts on every wing.

The daisies gossip, whisper low,
While roses flirt, a fragrant game,
The sunbeams dance with playful glow,
And nature's art just won't feel tame.

A butterfly with silly bends,
Flutters in, to steal the show,
It twirls and skims, and then pretends,
To be a kite in breezes slow.

With every scent and every shade,
The joy of bloom, each laugh, each cheer,
A palette bright, where fun's arrayed,
In nature's hands, we find our sphere.

Whispers of Sunlit Shores

On sandy beaches, crabs do waltz,
While sunburned tourists search for stalls.
A seagull steals a chip or two,
While locals laugh, "That's life for you!"

The coconut's a tricky chap,
It rolls away—oh what a trap!
A drink in hand, I spill and shout,
That's tropical life, without a doubt!

Flip-flops flying, what a sight,
As I take off, I'm gone in flight.
With sunblock stuck upon my nose,
I'm now a walking, laughing pose!

Beneath the palms, we take our rest,
From munching fruit to sun's caress.
In palm-leaf hats, we sip our drinks,
And chuckle loud, as everyone thinks!

Lush Breezes and Untamed Dreams

In jungles thick, we wander through,
Dodging bugs like ninjas do.
A toucan jokes, 'Hey! What's up?'
While swinging monkeys cheer and sup!

The lush green ferns tickle my toes,
As I trip over roots, that's how it goes.
A parrot squawks, 'You silly man!'
I give a grin, and thus I plan.

A wild retreat, with mist in air,
I find my hat stuck in a pair.
The breeze insists, it wants a dance,
While I'm here stuck in a prance!

The dreams we chase in tangled vines,
Are often lost, but that's just fine.
With laughter loud, we roam and laugh,
In nature's quirky, silly path!

Echoes of the Canopy

Up in the trees, the critters play,
Chasing each other, that's their way.
A sloth hangs low, so slow and sweet,
While squirrels giggle at his beat.

The echoes sing through leaves so green,
With whispered jokes we've never seen.
A vine wraps round my leg and stays,
And now it's part of my hair's new phase!

A toucan swoops, a colorful show,
I laugh and wonder, 'Where'd he go?'
The monkeys hoot a funny song,
They ask me if the time is wrong.

The forest floor, a wobbly dance,
As I trip over roots, not by chance.
But in this space, I find my cheer,
With nature's quirks, I have no fear!

Dance of the Parrots

Parrots twirl in a bright parade,
With every flap, they're unafraid.
'Come join us now!' they shout with glee,
Their feathered outfits—what a spree!

They squawk and squeak a silly tune,
While I compete with a friendly raccoon.
With goofy steps, we prance around,
In this tropical, joyous ground!

The iguanas join with style and flair,
As I attempt to dance with air.
A slip, a tumble, but what a laugh,
They clap their claws, I take a bow!

Each step we take, a message shared,
In silly moments, we're all prepared.
With chuckles bright, we sway away,
In this wild, tropical ballet!

Tropic Hues in the Dusk's Embrace

The sun dips low, a fiery ball,
A swimsuit tan just got too small.
With drinks in hand, we dance and sway,
The squawking birds join in our play.

Palm trees wiggle, what a sight,
They gossip softly, day and night.
An iguana dons a funky hat,
Glimpses of laughter make us chat.

As stars peek out to wink and shine,
We toast to laughs and sun-kissed wine.
The tropics giggle, join the fun,
With every joke, we loudly run.

So next time you need some cheer,
Just follow warmth, find a beer!
In hues of orange, pink, and gold,
The dusk embraces, daring, bold.

Where Solitude Meets the Song of Waves

Upon a shore, I saw a crab,
A silly dance, he wasn't drab.
He waved his claws, with flair and zest,
While seagulls shouted, 'Who's the best?'

The sunbathers snored in deep repose,
While fishy friends rehearsed their prose.
A wave would crash, a splash, a cheer,
'We're rehearsing for the big premiere!'

Here solitude plays a funky tune,
As shells debate beneath the moon.
The rhythm sways; they can't resist,
Join in the fun, you'll be missed!

So while I sit, mustlessly grinning,
The ocean laughs—what a beginning!
With every wave that rolls with glee,
In this small world, I'm fancy-free.

Shimmering Pathways to Paradise Found

A path of light, where laughter springs,
With flip-flop feet, we play like kings.
The coconut waves 'hello' at dawn,
While monkeys heckle like they're on.

Sandy toes and sun-kissed cheeks,
We hunt for treasures, it's what life seeks.
Sea turtles cheer us on with grace,
As we splash around—what a race!

Bright umbrellas bloom like flowers wide,
While ice cream drips, we laugh and glide.
Every bite's a tropical surprise,
With mango dreams and summer skies.

So follow the shimmer, take a chance,
Join in the waves, let your heart dance.
Paradise waits with arms spread wide,
In this funny journey, come for the ride.

The Secret Life of the Tropical Breeze

The breeze whispers secrets, oh so sly,
It tickles leaves, makes branches cry.
On lazy days, it plays hide and seek,
Where did it go? Come back, you sneak!

It carries laughter from tree to sea,
Mixing it up like a wild spree.
Tickling noses, swaying hips,
A dance party with shadowy flips!

From fragrant blooms, it lifts the scent,
Of sweetened fruits, with laughter bent.
Where children giggle and people sway,
The breeze nudges us, come out to play!

So listen closely, it's more than air,
In every gust, there's something rare.
When nature chuckles, and spirits tease,
Join the secret life of the breeze.

Serenade of the Singing Palms

In the breeze, the palms do sway,
Chirping birds join in the play.
Coconuts fall with a clunk!
"Who needs drums?" a parrot shrunk.

Sandy feet shuffle to the beat,
While crabs dance sideways, quite a feat.
Fish wear shades in the coral sea,
Singing, "Join us, it's free!"

Bikini tops waving like flags,
While sunburnt tourists look like rags.
A lizard tap-dances on the side,
As everyone here takes a ride.

With each giggle, the waves reply,
Palm trees sway to the sound of a sigh.
In this place, oh what a charm,
Even the sun won't cause you harm.

Sunlit Pathways Through Lush Paradise

Walking down these shady lanes,
Dodging squirrels with their silly gains.
A monkey chuckles from above,
Stealing snacks, oh how rude, my love!

Beneath the leaves, a lizard grins,
A dance-off starts; let's see who wins!
Mangoes tumble from trees like rain,
Slipping on juice? Dance through the pain!

Bright flowers gossip, colors ablaze,
Telling tales of the hottest craze.
A butterfly flutters; wears shades with style,
Tiny but sassy, oh, how it's worthwhile!

Flip-flops slapping, laughter trails behind,
Nature's groove is what we find.
Left or right? We'll just roam,
In this sunny place, we feel at home.

The Dance of Colors at Ocean's Edge

Waves don hats that float away,
As seagulls sport their beachy sway.
Fish do flips, oh what a sight,
Underwater parties start at night!

The ocean sings, a salty tune,
While sunbathers nap, counting to noon.
An octopus plays peek-a-boo,
Dancing shoes? They've got a few!

Towels bicker, flapping in the air,
While sunscreen spills like food to share.
Crabs in shades call everyone "dude!"
Setting the tone for a beachy mood.

Under the sun, the colors blend,
A canvas of laughter with no end.
In this shimmering world so fun,
Every moment shines bright like the sun.

Secrets of the Tropical Wilderness

Vines twist like gossip, secrets shared,
While parrots eye us, unprepared.
A sloth yawns, draped on a tree,
"Come back later, it's too hot for me!"

An iguana claims the best rock seat,
Sunglasses perched, feeling so neat.
Underneath, the frogs sing out loud,
Ribbit-ing on, drawing quite the crowd.

The jungle giggles, rustling each leaf,
"To explore or nap, that is the beef."
A toucan jests with a flamboyant beak,
Sharing stories, wild and sleek.

In this lush, green, humorous space,
Laughter echoes through every trace.
Join the fun, the whispers tease,
Tropical delights that always please.

Where the Ocean Meets the Sky

Seagulls squawk, doing aerial tricks,
While crabs dance in their little kicks,
Sunburned folks in a wild riot,
Building castles—oh, they get quiet!

Waves crash like jokes told too loud,
Flip-flops fly, they should be proud,
Sunsets sneak like a sneaky cat,
And dolphins giggle—imagine that!

Dreamscapes of Golden Sands

Tanning lotion, a slippery mess,
Sand stuck everywhere, what a stress!
Beach balls bounce with a squeaky thud,
While kids dig deep in a sandy flood.

The ice cream melts before you can lick,
Seagulls swoop in, oh, what a trick!
Sun hats flying like they have wings,
Join in the chaos, it's a goofy fling!

Tides of Endless Wanderlust

Travelers shuffle with bags galore,
Excited, they spill their snacks on the floor,
A map upside down, a confused sight,
With locals laughing, it's pure delight!

Bumpy roads lead to strange little huts,
While monkeys steal snacks, those sneaky nuts!
Sunburnt but happy, they wander near,
Each misadventure brings a hearty cheer!

Flickers of Fireflies Under Stars

Fireflies twinkle like stars on land,
And folks dance awkwardly, hand in hand,
Picnic blankets become a wild nest,
With ants hosting parties as the guests!

Laughter erupts like a soda pop,
As beach games tumble, and flip-flops plop,
A night so bright with lights all around,
Joyful moments in silliness found!

Chronicles of Colorful Feathers and Fins

Bright parrots squawk with cheer,
Trying to order a souvenir.
Fish in colors, loud and bold,
Wink at tales of treasures told.

Crabs dance sideways, what a sight,
In a disco, all through the night.
Turtles in ties, they glide and prance,
Inviting all to join the dance.

Lemonade spills, too sweet to sip,
Sticky fingers on a joyride trip.
Sandy feet in flip-flops chase,
Seagulls stealing food at a fast pace.

Under stars, under a clam-filled moon,
Laughter echoes, a merry tune.
Island friends share fishy grime,
With jokes that feel like sunny rhyme.

Breathing Life into Tropical Enchantment

Coconuts bob on waves of glee,
Monkeys swing, so wild and free.
Banana peels fly in the air,
Landing right on grandma's chair.

Palm trees lean, they shake and sway,
As if to say, 'Come out and play!'
Frogs in chorus, sing so spry,
One claims he can touch the sky.

A colorful parade of bugs passes by,
Each one hoping to win a prize.
A lizard in glasses, far too cool,
Sips on nectar like a summer school.

With smiles broad, time drifts along,
A playful world, where no one's wrong.
Joy spills out, a vibrant show,
In a land where giggles grow.

A Symphony of Sights and Sounds

Dancing waves have a tune to share,
While the crabs practice their jive with flair.
The breeze giggles through the palm fronds,
As lizards plot their next pooly responds.

Sunshine plays tag, a vibrant game,
Chasing shadows without any shame.
Frisky monkeys throw mangoes high,
Landing right where it makes folks sigh.

Parrots echo with a cheeky tease,
"What's your name? Come join the breeze!"
Sailboats laugh as they glide past,
While the wind warns of a storm too fast.

Yet here we stay, a merry clan,
With flippers, fins, we'll make our plan.
To swim and leap, to giggle loud,
In this parody, we're quite proud.

The Invisible Ties of Island Kin

A hammock swings with thoughts so bright,
As sunsets paint the sky with light.
Cousins gather, sharing each tale,
Making memories that will never pale.

Fishy stories filled with spice,
Who caught the biggest, who caught the slice?
Grandmas dance with canes held high,
While grandkids roll and attempt to fly.

Potlucks smelling of tropical stew,
Though nobody knows exactly who.
Laughter arises, plates piled high,
With a dash of chaos that can't deny.

As stars twinkle like giggles spun,
The night grows old, but never done.
Linked by laughter down to our shoes,
In island tales, there's always news.

Embrace of the Warm Winds.

In the sun, my ice cream melts,
I run fast like a kid, so it felt.
Dancing like a palm tree's sway,
Not a care till the end of the day.

Flip-flops squeak with each bold step,
In sandy shoes, I've lost my prep.
Crabs steal my lunch—oh what a heist!
Now I'm left with just rice and spice.

A parrot laughed, what a crazy squawk,
It mimicked my dance and my talk.
With piña coladas, we toast to cheer,
To this wacky life, full of joy and beer.

As night falls, the stars begin their show,
While I trip on the beach and go slow.
Under the moon, I'll trip and I'll spin,
This warmth and fun, oh let's do it again!

Emerald Dreams of Distant Shores

Where the waves crash and giggle bright,
I dream of surfing with all my might.
But each attempt turns into a flop,
As I belly-flop, and then I stop.

Seagulls dive-bomb, ready for a feast,
I throw my chips; they're hungry, at least.
In this paradise where I feel free,
And they laugh as much as they tease me.

Coconuts roll like balls in play,
While I sip my drink and sunbathe away.
I wear a hat, it's way too wide,
But it's my shield from the sun's hot ride.

At night, the crickets join the band,
With their tunes, they make the night grand.
I dance with shadows, twirl with glee,
Emerald dreams, forever with me.

Whispers of the Island Breeze

In the hammock, I start to sway,
The breeze whispers secrets, playful and gay.
It tickles my toes, makes my hair fly,
As I wonder if it's magic or pie.

The lizards giggle, they're in on the joke,
While I chase them, trying not to choke.
With every slip on the sandy ground,
The island smiles, its joy unbound.

A sunburnt nose is a badge of pride,
As I lounge and let the troubles slide.
The fish in the sea wave a fin or two,
While I compete for the sun with my brew.

In this paradise, laughter fills the air,
With each silly moment, all worries I bear.
The whispers wrap around, soft as a feather,
It's a life of joy, oh, let's laugh together!

Beneath the Canopy's Caress

Under leaves, where the sunlight peeks,
I munch on fruits, oh, what a treat!
The monkeys giggle, I slip on a vine,
This jungle party is simply divine.

Beneath the branches, I find my groove,
As bugs perform, making me move.
With every hop, I leap and I laugh,
An unplanned trip on a tree's tough path.

Loud frogs croak, putting on a show,
While I try to dance, and end in a low.
The fireflies flicker, stars come alive,
In this funny jungle, we all thrive.

At dusk, the night brings a magical charm,
As I fall in a pile, it's all quite warm.
With laughter echoing under the sky,
Beneath the canopy, I'm ready to fly.

Tales from the Winding River

In a boat that squeaks and sways,
Ducklings laugh, with no delays.
A fish jumps high, a splashy leap,
Splashing me, I yelp and weep.

Bamboos dance with breezy cheer,
A crocodile gives me a sneer.
I tell a joke, but he just grins,
As mosquitoes buzz for evening wins.

Overhead, the parrots chatter,
I can't hear, what's that clatter?
They mimic me, it makes me fall,
I wave goodbye, they call and call.

As the sun sinks low, I cheer my fate,
With a fishy tale to narrate.
The ripples giggle, the river's wide,
And I paddle on with silly pride.

Island Hues and Breath of Salt

On an island where colors collide,
A parrot painted, took me for a ride.
He squawked a tune, misplaced the beat,
I danced around, tripping my feet.

The coconuts roll, a game we play,
Falling down, they just won't stay.
A monkey laughs with a banana grin,
I throw him a shell, he throws it in.

The waves come in with a goofy splash,
I dive right in, it's a belly crash.
Seashells giggle, as I roam around,
With salty hair, there's joy unbound.

As the sunset glows, painting the sky,
With laughter and joy, I wave goodbye.
To this island of hues, it's a silly scene,
Where fun never ends and I live like a queen.

Spirits in the Misty Morning

In the mist, I stub my toe,
A ghostly laugh, 'Oh no, oh no!'
The trees whisper secrets, maybe some lies,
As I squint through fog, with sleepy eyes.

With my coffee, I seek the blame,
For spooking myself, it's always the same.
A shadow dances, glides by fast,
I trip again, 'Will this ever last?'

The cuckoo calls, a cheeky jest,
I think it's mocking my morning quest.
A wisp of wind gives me a shove,
"Not now, dear spirits, I'm not in the mood for love!"

But giggling mist wraps around tight,
As I wander and fumble with all my might.
The dawn chuckles, "Oh silly, you see?
In this fog-filled morning, it's just you and me!"

Vibrations of Distant Drums

From afar, the drums begin to play,
Their funky beats just sweep me away.
I sway to the left, then the right,
My dancing's a sight, oh what a fright!

With every beat, I lose my shoes,
Spinning and twirling, oh what to lose?
The crabs clap claws, laughing in sync,
As I trip on the sand, and pause to think.

Around the bonfire, spirits ignite,
They join in my dance, a funny sight.
The stars are giggling, the moon rolls his eyes,
As I play my part in this shambolic surprise.

But when the drumming fades into night,
I tumble and laugh, at my own silly plight.
With memories echoing, I wave at the sun,
"Till next drumbeat, oh what fun!"

Elysium Found in the Tropics' Heart

In a hammock hung beneath a tree,
A coconut fell, oh dear me!
It rolled and bounced, a wild spree,
Claiming my drink, now that's not key!

The sunbeams teasing my sunburnt nose,
I danced with crabs who wear fine clothes.
They showed me moves in their sandy glows,
But I tripped on shells, now that's how it goes!

Parrots squawk secrets, loud and clear,
Mocking my laughter as I draw near.
They mimic my thoughts, oh what a fear,
A feathered comedian, my tropical peer!

Yet amidst this chaos, joy takes flight,
With fruity drinks and laughter's delight.
Elysium's heart feels so right,
In this raucous realm, my dreams ignite!

A Tidal Dance of Shadows and Light

Waves crash and whisper secrets profound,
Surfboards spin, oh what a sound!
The fish pop up, all around,
They laugh at my skills, I feel so drowned!

The sun dips low, a fiery friend,
But my sunscreen's failed, it won't defend.
I gleam like a lobster, a tropical trend,
A comical sight that none can suspend!

Shells dance in tide, in rhythm they sway,
I try to join in, but soon lose my way.
Tidal ballet, come join this play,
As I juggle sand, what a glorious display!

Night falls, stars emerge in the dance,
I slip and slide, but still take a chance.
In the moon's light, I twirl and prance,
The ocean laughs, this is fate's romance!

Guardians of the Emerald Paradise

Monkeys in capes, they guard the trees,
Swinging around with goofy glee.
They throw their snacks—a sight to seize,
While I dodge falling fruit, oh please!

Lush greens swirl, a vibrant show,
But I lost my hat in the wind's wild blow.
The creatures chuckle as I bumble low,
In emerald realms, I'm just a slow-go!

Each leaf a story, each branch a tale,
Parrots recounting how I did fail.
I mimic back, but they'll prevail,
With shrieks of laughter on the tropical trail!

So here's to the guardians, quite the team,
In this paradise, life's a dream.
With every blunder, they plot and scheme,
Emerald laughter—what a wild theme!

Waves Whispering Secrets to the Stars

Under the moon, the waves begin to tease,
I try to dance, but my feet just freeze.
The ocean giggles, a gentle breeze,
With every misstep, it's pure unease!

The stars watch on as I flail and flop,
A fish leaps out, it'll never stop.
"Join the fun!" they say, "It's quite the hop!"
But I splash in water, oh what a drop!

Turtles glide by in a slow-motion race,
I'm in awe of their peaceful pace.
But when I join in, I lose my grace,
A beach bum stranded, what a disgrace!

Yet, in this laughter, joy is the norm,
With nature's whimsy, my heart will warm.
In this chaotic dance, I'm part of the swarm,
Waves whisper secrets, a life so warm!

Under the Gaze of a Gentle Sun

Sandy toes in bright blue seas,
Sunburned noses in the breeze.
Lemonade with rum, oh wow!
Let's dance like parrots, here and now!

Coconuts drop with raucous thuds,
While we laugh and roll in the suds.
Flip-flops flying, what a sight!
Who knew that fun could take this flight?

Sunsets spill like melted gold,
At this age, we still feel bold.
With each guffaw and gleeful shout,
We live life large, no room for doubt!

Under stars that wink and beam,
Even the crabs join in our dream.
Here's to joy, let's raise a cheer,
In this slice of paradise, oh dear!

Journey Through a Tropical Wonderland

Boarding a boat with a squeaky sound,
Just hope the fish won't drag me down.
With hats too big, we set the sail,
And giggle as we tell a tale.

The beach is a stage, oh what a show!
Flopping like seals, we steal the glow.
With sunscreen thick as cake icing,
Our laughter is truly enticing!

Island hops and mango whip,
Tasting all things that make us flip.
Squawking birds look on in glee,
As we hula, wild and free!

Every sunset spills its paint,
With colors that could make one faint.
And in our hearts, we keep this tune,
Forever dancing by the moon.

A Tapestry Woven with Nature's Threads

In a hammock strung between two trees,
I wonder if the bugs are pleased.
The sun's a joker, always bright,
And every breeze, a soft delight.

Fruity hats and sandals bold,
We flaunt our styles, a sight to behold!
Laughter echoes through flowered scents,
The whole world seems to make no sense!

Palm leaves dance in gentle sway,
As birds plot their mischief in play.
It's silly, but we feel so grand,
We'd rather fake a marching band!

Even the critters join our spree,
A chorus of chirps in harmony.
With each day brimming with jest,
Nature spins its merry fest!

Midnight Serenades in Paradise

Under stars, the party sways,
As crickets sing the night away.
Mango pies and tropical twists,
In mischief's grasp, we can't resist!

A fire pit where shadows prance,
With every story, we take a chance.
Marshmallows roasting like cheeky friends,
The sweet aroma never ends.

Moonlight dances, steals the scene,
In this wonderland, we feel like kings.
With seashells clinking, laughter's free,
What a life, sly as can be!

Toasting dreams with fizzy pops,
With every giggle, good mood hops.
In the night, we lose all dread,
And drift with joy on laughter's bread!

A Canvas Painted with Life's Brush

In a hammock I sway, with a drink in my hand,
My worries dissolve like sugar in sand.
The sun has a grin, the sky wears a hue,
It's hard to be serious when the birds squawk their view.

Pineapples giggle as they dance on the trees,
While coconuts tumble; watch out for these!
The beach is like laughter, it tickles my toes,
Each wave brings a chuckle; oh, what fun it bestows!

Crabs in a lineup, strutting their stuff,
With tiny sunglasses and a move that's quite tough.
The seagulls are gossiping, their tales full of sass,
While I munch on a taco, hoping this moment will last.

So here's to the hues of the sea and the sun,
Where every bright day is bursting with fun.
A canvas of laughter, where life likes to play,
In this wacky paradise, I could stay every day!

Coastal Whispers and Island Wishes

The breeze brings a giggle, the waves clap their hands,
As I chase after crabs, making silly plans.
The palm trees are swaying, they dance with the sun,
While I try to keep up, but oh, what a run!

A parrot is squawking, giving weather reports,
In a language of chuckles, as he fluffs up his shorts.
The tide rolls in laughter, all frothy and bright,
While I slip on a shell, and I'm shooting out like a kite!

Flip-flops are flopping, my style—oh so grand,
I'm the fashion icon of this sandy land.
With a bucket for treasure, I seek out the fun,
Digging up memories, I'm not the only one!

So here's to the chirps and the splashes of glee,
To the shenanigans brought by this bright, breezy sea.
With each coastal whisper that tickles my ear,
Every moment spent here, I hold oh-so-dear!

Gathering Storms Over Tropical Valleys

In valleys wide, the clouds do dance,
They rumble low, a daring chance.
A monkey swings, a coconut flies,
Oh, what a scene beneath stormy skies!

Lizards leap with comic grace,
While raindrops fall, a splashing race.
The thunder claps, but fears take flight,
As nature laughs, oh what a sight!

Bananas bicker in the breeze,
While palm trees sway with perfect ease.
A parrot squawks some silly cheer,
As storm clouds roll, we hold them dear!

Yet when the rain begins to play,
A wild fiesta steals the day.
In nature's jest, we find our fun,
The storm sings loud, we join as one!

Forests of Laughter and Light

In forests thick, where shadows creep,
The critters giggle, not a peep.
A sloth with style, moves like a pro,
While squirrels tease him, 'Come on, go!'

Bright butterflies wear vibrant hats,
And dance around the playful gnats.
A toucan smiles with fruit in beak,
His jokes are bold, his charm unique!

Amid the trees, a party swells,
With frogs that croak their ribbit spells.
The sunlight sparkles, laughter rings,
In nature's room, it's joy that sings!

So wander here, where mirth is found,
In every blink, joy knows no bound.
Through laughter's maze, let's take our flight,
In forests bright, by laughter's light!

A Food for the Soul in Tropic Sanctuaries

In orchards ripe, the sweetness grows,
Bananas hang in cheerful rows.
A monkey munches, grinning wide,
While fruit bats join the joyful ride!

The papayas boast their golden hue,
With every bite, a giggly chew.
Pineapples wear crowns, oh so grand,
They joke about the unripe band!

A coconut rolls, a playful tease,
While hungry ants swarm with such ease.
The mangoes muse, 'We're the best!',
In this sweet world, who's less and blessed?

So come and taste what joy can glean,
In every fruit, a funny scene.
A sanctuary where flavors dance,
Let's savor life, and take a chance!

Sunkissed Moments in a Vibrant World

Under the sun, the world's aglow,
Where laughter bubbles, a constant flow.
In every nook, a giggle waits,
As colors burst through laughter's gates.

The sandy shores, with crabs that prance,
They shuffle sideways, give us a chance.
A beach ball bounces, ducks in rows,
As children giggle, the wind it blows!

Rooftops sprout with laughter's cheer,
As sun-kissed days draw us near.
Watermelons roll down the lane,
In this bright world, there's no room for pain!

So join the dance in vibrant haze,
Let humor bloom in sunny rays.
In moments sweet, where life's a swirl,
We laugh and play in this bright world!

Echoes of Laughter Along Sandy Trails

Footprints giggle in the sand,
Crabs dance with a funny band.
Coconuts tell jokes at noon,
While lizards strut, they start to croon.

Palm trees whisper secrets bold,
As the sun turns folks to gold.
With each wave, a chuckle swells,
Nature shares her amusing tales.

Flip-flops squeak, a comic sound,
Over towels, laughter's found.
Seagulls squawk in cheerful tones,
A beachy orchestra of phones.

Under skies that bubble bright,
Every moment feels just right.
Laughter echoes, now and then,
On sandy trails, we dream again.

Fading Footprints in Warm Sands

Footprints fade as tides come near,
Each one brings a burst of cheer.
Sandcastles lean, they seem to wink,
Giggling crabs are quick to think.

Kids throw beach balls, watch them fly,
Only to see them hit a pie.
Splashes follow, wet and wild,
As laughter reigns, both free and styled.

Sunscreen fights become a game,
Squeaky screams, we're all to blame.
Flip-flops fly from running feet,
Hiding treasures, oh what a feat!

The shoreline's full of funny sights,
In bright colors and joyful lights.
With every wave, a new surprise,
Smiles grow wide, while laughter flies.

Lush Horizons Under Endless Skies

Colorful birds sing silly tunes,
While monkeys swing and act like loons.
Bananas wear a crown so bright,
And giggles fill the air with light.

Palm fronds dance, exposing flair,
As folks break out in joyous air.
Bamboo boats tip, then laugh away,
Chasing mischief on the bay.

Fields of flowers, swaying near,
Invite butterflies with cheer.
Bees buzz jokes from bloom to bloom,
While flowers giggle, scent the room.

Under skies that seem to grin,
Join the fun, let joy begin.
Waves and whispers all around,
In nature's playground, joy is found.

Rituals of Rain and Sunlight

Rain falls down in playful beats,
Puddles bounce with funny feats.
When the sun peeks through the gray,
Splashes turn to dancing play.

Umbrellas flip, a crazy sight,
As folks attempt to dodge the light.
Slip and slide in joyous glee,
Nature's game, just wait and see.

Colors pop, rainbows ignite,
In this world where fun feels right.
Coconut drinks spill with a splash,
Twist and twirl, oh what a dash!

The rhythm of beads in the wet,
Is a tune we won't forget.
Laughing under sun or rain,
These rituals, a sweet refrain.

Embracing the Spirit of Warmth

In sun-kissed lands where coconuts sway,
Parrots laugh loud, in their colorful play.
Flip-flops and laughter, we dance in the sand,
Where sunscreen's applied by a toddler's hand.

She fell in a pool, just a jump from the shore,
Sirens sang sweetly, as she begged for no more.
But sunbeams are cheeky, they catch you off guard,
With sunburned noses that look a bit hard.

Ice cream melts fast, drips down to our feet,
We giggle and chase it, a sticky retreat.
While leaping in laughter, the waves start to tease,
A tropical tide that brings joy with the breeze.

So let's raise a toast with our fruity delight,
To bites of adventure that feel just right.
In places so silly, we'll always belong,
In warmth and in giggles, we'll sing our own song.

The Palette of a Sun-Filled Day

A canvas so bright, splashed with hues so bold,
A pineapple dances, its story unfolds.
With shades of the sunset, we swim through a dream,
Where laughter's the brush, and joy's the scheme.

We paint with our smoothies, the seas turn to blue,
Each sip a delight, oh, who needs a brew?
The beach ball's a rebel, it flies through the air,
And children chase giggles, not a single care.

With sun hats askew, and beach games so swift,
In sandcastle kingdoms, our imaginations lift.
Dunking each other, all squeals and delight,
As seagulls join in on our fun-filled fight.

The world is a masterpiece, vibrant and loud,
With colorful moments, let's gather a crowd.
So grab your brush softly, let fun colors sway,
In this playful paradise, life's a grand display.

Exploring the Heart of the Green Abyss

Through jungles of laughter, we wander with glee,
Where monkeys wear sunglasses, oh what do we see?
A lizard in disco, all ready to groove,
While sloths cheer him on, with a very slow move.

The vines tell us tales, of old leaves and dreams,
Where puddles are mirrors reflecting our schemes.
With raincoats for fashion, we splash through the glade,
While giggling at frogs wearing hats that we made.

But beware of the tickles, from leaves that might tease,
As vines with a sense of humor rustle the breeze.
Explorer or comedian, who knows where it ends?
In this green world of wonder, we're all budding friends.

So let's dance through the ferns, with make-believe flights,
Chasing the sunbeams that flicker like lights.
In this wild, wacky jungle, we jump and we sway,
Finding joy in the quirks, come on, let's play!

Time Stands Still in Tropical Refuge

In a hammock so cozy, we nap through the noon,
With the soft rustle of leaves and a sweet, lazy tune.
The world can wait kindly, there's nothing to rush,
As breezes bring whispers, and palm fronds all hush.

A piña colada, it calls to my side,
While flamingos waltz, in a fanciful stride.
With monkeys as jesters, they swing to the beat,
While we sit here chuckling, life's simple and sweet.

The clocks hold their breath, in this paradise fine,
Where flip-flops are worn like a badge of divine.
The crabs make us giggle, as they dance on the shore,
In this timeless retreat, who could ask for more?

So let's throw away worries, with pebbles and shells,
Where laughter just echoes and sunshine compels.
With toes in the water, we bask in the fun,
In this joyful oasis, forever we run.

The Symphony of Life in Bloom

In a jungle where the monkeys swing,
Lizards dance, and birds all sing,
A parrot squawks, great comedic flair,
Telling jokes like he just doesn't care.

Frogs croak tunes that make you laugh,
While flowers bloom; it's a riotous gaffe,
Sunshine tickles the vibrant scene,
Life bursts forth with a vibrant sheen.

The bees buzz round, wearing tiny hats,
While flowers blush like bashful chats,
Everyone's joining in this spree,
Where laughter drips like honey tea.

Oh, what a show! The jungle's stage,
As critters perform; it's all the rage,
With every beat and each silly sound,
Here, joy in abundance can always be found.

Reflections Beneath a Coconut Canopy

Underneath the palm fronds swaying high,
A crab attempts to be a butterfly,
It sidesteps clumsily, what a sight,
Dreaming of wings, oh what a plight!

Coconuts drop with a comical thud,
Sending critters into playful mudd,
Squeals of laughter echo on the shore,
As sea turtles take a tumble and roar.

A sunburnt tourist fumbles his drink,
Trying to focus, he starts to blink,
While local kids start a coconut toss,
Laughing hard, as they gain the gloss.

The shadows play tricks on the fun-loving crowd,
As giggles ripple through the palm leaves loud,
In this paradise where silliness reigns,
Life reflects joy, washing away all pains.

Breath of the Tropics in Every Leaf

Beneath the leafy shades, so green,
A sloth moves slowly, a living machine,
With great deliberation, he munches on vines,
While the toucan cackles and reads the signs.

Ferns wave their hands like they're saying hi,
While butterflies flit with a gleeful sigh,
Lizards blink twice, "What's all the fuss?"
In a world that spins without much fuss.

The breeze carries whispers from critters unseen,
"Who's got the snacks?" is their constant scene,
Laughter erupts from the fragrant blooms,
As the woodland dances, shaking off glooms.

Each leaf seems to giggle in the breeze,
Sharing secrets with the buzzing bees,
Where mirth is a breath, free and naive,
In this vibrant world, you learn to believe.

Shadows of Paradise Lost and Found

In the twilight where shadows begin to play,
Lizards meditate on the end of the day,
As the sun dips low, it turns things funny,
With silhouettes shaped like dancing honey.

A pineapple rolls like it's found a friend,
While mangoes argue, "We're the latest trend!"
In the twilight glow, all worries fade,
As crickets provide the night serenade.

Coconuts whisper sweet nothings, it's true,
To a coconut crab who thinks he's a shoe,
And if you listen, the waves have a laugh,
At all the antics that dance down the path.

Lost in this paradise, stories abound,
Every shadow hides laughter, tightly wound,
The night reveals what the day can't unmask,
In this laughter-filled place, who needs to ask?

The Lure of Swaying Palms

Beneath the palm trees, I do dance,
With coconuts swaying, they take a chance.
The monkeys swing by, they throw a laugh,
As I trip on my towel, what a gaffe!

The sun's so bright, my fries start to fry,
I've lost my hat; oh where did it fly?
A seagull swoops in, it steals my snack,
"Hey buddy, come back!" I shout with a crack.

The breeze brings scents of sunscreen and lime,
I try to relax, but it's quite a climb.
My kids are building, a castle of sand,
And now I'm stuck, just like a lost band!

I raise my drink, it's fruity and bright,
But then a big wave comes! What a fright!
With laughter and splashes, we embrace the sun,
In this tropical chaos, we always have fun.

Secrets of the Jungle Heart

In the jungle, where the monkeys play,
I planned to hike, but they led me astray.
With vines all around, I stumbled in glee,
A bushy-tailed lizard laughed right at me!

The sloths move slowly, they take their sweet time,
While I try to keep pace, it feels like a crime.
I saw a huge snake with its tongue all a-flick,
"Is it a pet?" I asked, feeling quite sick!

A toucan swoops in, its beak like a song,
It screams "You don't belong! Come dance along!"
So I twirl and I shimmy, forget about fear,
Until I trip over roots; oh dear, oh dear!

From bugs that can bite to plants that can sting,
Each twist and each turn makes my head start to swing.
But laughter erupts, it's a jungle parade,
With giggles and grins, we'll never fade.

Symphony of Colorful Shores

Oh, the shores that shimmer, oh what a sight,
With beach balls a-bouncing, it's pure delight!
I brought my old boogie board, what a ride,
Now I'm face-first in sand, oh what a pride!

My flip-flops are missing, they float on the tide,
While seagulls are laughing, I can't run and hide.
There's sunscreen on my nose, like a clown in a show,
I wave at my friends; "No, it's not a bow!"

With kids making castles, I'm summoned to help,
But somehow it seems I've trapped a fine kelp.
The sea turtles cheer as I dig and I dig,
I think I'm the king, a real beachy bigwig!

As the sun starts to set, the colors ignite,
I dance to the waves, feeling light as a kite.
With giggles and splashes, the day fades to night,
In this funny paradise, everything feels right.

Horizon of Endless Horizons

The horizon stretches, oh what a show,
A flamingo skates by – "Hey, look at me go!"
With my partner in sunblock, we squint at the breeze,
But the sun loves to sneak; it plays with such ease.

At this endless expanse, our worries swim free,
But I forgot my hat—oh, silly me!
A crab scuttles by, giving me a gaze,
As if to say, "Friend, don't enter my maze!"

Kites float above, like jellyfish wild,
I'm caught in their strings—oh, where is that child?
With laughter erupting, we race on the sand,
Our towels a beacon, our sunscreen the brand!

As dusk paints the sky with colors so bold,
We tell all our tales, both funny and old.
With waves in the backdrop and giggles in store,
This horizon of ours is never a bore!

Collected Stories of the Seaside

Seagulls squawk and steal my fries,
Sunburned tourists in funny ties.
Sandcastles crumble, a flop, a fail,
A crab waves bye, it's set to sail.

Turtles wearing shades stroll the sand,
Chasing flip-flops that kids have planned.
Beach balls bounce like they're alive,
Daring each kid to take a dive.

Ice cream drips, a melting mess,
Sticky hands in a summer dress.
A dog steals a beach hat, oh what fun,
Life by the sea can't be outdone.

At dusk, a dance of the beach lights,
Fishermen sing with seafood bites.
Laughter echoes, waves on the roam,
Who needs a house when sand is home?

Awakened by the Murmurs of the Shore

Waves whisper tales, sweet and strange,
Some fish ask if we've had a change.
Flipping flops and sandy toes,
Who needs shoes when the surf glows?

Crabs host parties with shells for chairs,
While seagulls practice their funny stares.
A jellyfish wears a jaunty hat,
As sunbathers lie like cats in a mat.

The tide brings in a floating shoe,
"Where's the other?" we all ask too.
Octopuses juggle with flair and grace,
While kids dip toes, a splash, a chase.

Evening sets with a burst of cheer,
As stars peek out, the night is near.
Seaside we laugh, lose track of time,
Dance with the waves, in beats and rhyme.

Ships of Dreams in Calm Waters

A rubber duck sails on a breeze,
Claiming oceans with perfect ease.
Captain of bubbles, on patrol,
While sharks swim by, not wanting a role.

Old boats creak like they know secrets,
Reminiscing their oceanic feats.
A parrot squawks about steak and fries,
While fishes giggle through watery sighs.

On calm shores, a pirate appears,
With a treasure map made of frozen cheers.
X marks the spot under a palm,
Where sunbakers lay all free and calm.

Every wave knows a sailor's song,
Even the seahorses weave along.
Life on the water, a greedy dream,
Where nothing is quite what it might seem.

Portraits of Sunset and Coconut Trees

A sunset spills paint across the sky,
While roosters crow and seagulls fly.
Coconut hatted folks take their place,
As waves start to dance with untamed grace.

Palm trees sway, hairpin versions of cool,
While beachgoers sip from a shell-shaped pool.
Sunscreens mixed with sand makes a blend,
Each reluctant goodbye is a funny trend.

A cat takes the sun, claims it as throne,
With a crown of leaves, a true beach drone.
Flip-flops flapping, a comical race,
As nighttime wraps the day's wild embrace.

Mismatched socks declare fashion's fun,
Laughter and joy—we're never done.
In festive hues, the horizon gleams,
As midnight whispers of sandy dreams.

Tides of Jade and Crystal Waters

The waves danced like they had shoes,
While crabs cranked jokes with the sea blues.
An octopus juggled in splendid view,
Saying, 'I'd join the circus, but I'm stuck in goo!'

The coconut palms were in a fierce debate,
About who's the tallest, oh isn't that great?
The sand was a beach, but it had its say,
'You wobbly waves, just go home and play!'

Seagulls were gossiping, landing with flair,
Complaining 'bout shrimp, always under their care.
And fish in formation swam by in a whirl,
Making mermaids giggle, oh what a swirl!

With each splash of laughter, the shores knew delight,
As turtles performed, oh what a sight!
In jade and crystal, their shenanigans flow,
In this seaside circus, the fun's on a roll!

Melodies of the Moonlit Lagoon

Under the moon, frogs shot their best jams,
While fireflies danced in tiny light flams.
Cattails joined in with a quaint little beat,
While otters played maracas with colorful feet.

The night was alive with a symphony wild,
As crickets chirped softly; nature's own child.
A turtle DJ mixed tunes with a smile,
Saying, 'Let's keep this grooving for a while!'

Fish in the water did the backstroke with ease,
Echoing giggles blown by the breeze.
And as the stars twinkled, they shone with delight,
Making sure every creature was dancing tonight.

The lagoon held a carnival, laughter in rows,
Where dreams took wing and fancy arose.
In ripples of joy, they sang all night long,
A chorus of life, where everyone belongs!

Currents of Adventure in Exotic Lands

In lands where the llamas wore hats so refined,
And parrots told tales to the bears, oh so kind.
The rivers were giggling, twisting and turning,
With fish playing tag and the sun brightly burning.

A monkey gave high-fives, swinging through trees,
While a sloth told a story, as slow as you please.
'Hey, buddy!' said the snake, 'You're missing the show!'

'Relax,' said the sloth, 'I'm part of the flow.'

The sun spilled its colors on each little stream,
Every creature found fun, igniting their dream.
So as each adventure would unfold in the sand,
They'd laugh with the sea and dance hand in hand!

In exotic lands, where silliness reigns,
Each ripple, each smile, by friendship gains.
With currents of laughter, they rode every wave,
In a whirlwind of joy, oh how it's brave!

Flora's Embrace in Radiant Glades

In glades where the flowers wore dresses all bright,
The daisies were swaying, oh what a sight!
Butterflies burst out in fabulous dance,
While bumblebees buzzed in a floral romance.

A cheeky dandelion wiggled its head,
Saying, 'I'm famous, now everyone's spread!'
The violets giggled, blue shades on display,
While roses shouted, 'Hey, join our bouquet!'

The sunflowers joked, 'We're the height of the game!'
Each petal expressed, 'Oh, we're not the same!'
In radiant glades, where bright colors cheer,
The flora embraced all, spreading joy far and near.

Through whispers of laughter, the flowers would sing,
Inviting all creatures to join in the fling.
So come join the fun, in this garden so grand,
Where merriment flourishes, all hand in hand!

Beneath a Tropical Sky

Beneath a sky with hues so bright,
Where flip-flops dance and sunburns bite.
The coconuts hang with jokester glee,
While crabs compete in a wacky spree.

A parrot squawks, oh what a tease,
He steals your sandwich with perfect ease.
Laughter echoes on sandy shores,
As beach balls roll and laughter soars.

The sun is hot; we wear a grin,
Though sunscreen's missing, we let it win.
A surfboard challenge, oh what fun!
I'm wiped out, but who's got the sun?

So here we lie, on towels spread wide,
With ice cream cones and a churning tide.
We giggle loud, with joy we gleam,
Beneath this sky, we live the dream.

Serenade of the Palm Trees

Oh, listen close to the rustling leaves,
As palm trees sway, plotting mischief up their sleeves.
They whisper secrets to the ocean breeze,
While monkeys munch on ripe bananas with ease.

With every swing, they crack a joke,
As gopher turtles in sunbaths croak.
A beach ball bounces, what a sight,
As it hits the palm, takes flight, oh what might!

Flip-flops slapping like a maraca beat,
As we cha-cha towards the nearest treat.
The coconuts laugh when fall they do,
Claiming, "Look out! I've got a surprise for you!"

This serenade of tropical fun,
A laughter symphony under the sun.
With each breeze, our spirits rise,
The palm trees chuckle, oh what a surprise!

Mysteries of the Coral Depths

In coral reefs where fish do glide,
A clownfish dances, who's on the slide?
The turtle looks on, scratching his chin,
As seaweed tickles, who'll win this din?

Jellyfish float like wobbly marshmallows,
While dolphins play leapfrog, oh what fellows!
A conch shell giggles, what could it say?
"Stop tickling me, save some for play!"

The octopus waves with a stylish flair,
While sea urchins grin without a care.
Anemones sway, like they're in a band,
Making music, oh how they expand!

So dive on down, see the ruckus unfold,
In the depths of mysteries, adventures untold.
With sea creatures laughing and bubbles that pop,
You'll find joy in the depths, now let's hop!

Vibrant Nights and Moonlit Tides

At dusk, the stars begin to play,
With fireflies bursting, lighting the way.
Tiki torches flicker, what a sight!
As laughter spills into the warm night.

The moon hums softly, casting her light,
While crickets chirp in exclusive delight.
Beach blankets spread, a laughter parade,
With stories of clumsiness serenely laid.

Salty snacks twinkle like stars in their bowl,
As we feast and giggle, what a fun goal!
With waves that splash and moonbeams that glide,
We dance and we stumble, joy as our guide.

So under the sun-kissed skies that collide,
We toast to the nights, let joy be our ride.
In vibrant moments, let silliness bloom,
As moonlit tides echo our laughter and room.

www.ingramcontent.com/pod-product-compliance
Lightning Source LLC
Chambersburg PA
CBHW072131070526
44585CB00016B/1626